Parenting: Keep it Simple & Do it Right

by Bill Edwards

About The Author

Bill Edwards is a professional writer, author, speaker, business consultant and life skills expert in his fifties. Bill has appeared on many national and international radio shows, television and web broadcasts, and been featured in a number of well-known newspapers, periodicals and publications.

Introduction

It took me many years to try and assemble a book about Parenting that included what I felt were the best and most successful ideas for and methods of child rearing. Having successfully raised seven children and been married to the same wonderful woman for the past twenty-eight years, I definitely wanted to include our solutions to common problems that all parents face at one time or another.

I also had a desire to make sure that my book included practical advice that I have received from legitimate experts who not only know what they are talking about, but have actually helped people with all sorts of parenting issues. What I did not want was for my book to be 'preachy' or give readers the impression that they were going to have to muddle their way through yet another parenting book with all kinds of politically correct and touchy-feely ideas that simply do not work in real life.

'Parenting: Keep it Simple & Do it Right' is designed to be a practical guide to parenting problems and real life solutions that any parent in any situation will find helpful. It is not overly wordy, long-winded or complicated. I kept the language simple and the content pure. I left out all the adjectives and wrote this book without the usual self ego inflating style that I have found in far too many other self-help titles. I trust that this book and what's inside will work as well for you as it has for me and many others.

Chapter One: Parenting: Myths and The Truth About Breast Feeding

Bare breasts have always interested babies and men, but now they are being used to promote everything from fringe parenting methods to cookies. Cases in point: A recent Time Magazine cover features a fully clothed woman with what appears to be one breast exposed for the purpose of breast feeding her four year son; yes I did say her four year old son. Another photo is part of an ad campaign in South Korea and shows an infant feeding on a woman's breast. The ad is for Oreo Cookies and features the caption, "Milk's favorite cookie. Oreo."

Before I get going on all of this I want to be fair. Breast feeding older children, especially males, is a cultural phenomenon in many Asia countries and other places around the globe. That said, I do not live in an Asian country and there comes a time when someone has to stand up to what amounts to an almost passive, but harmful form of child abuse. There are many reasons not to breast feed children past the age of one or two years.

I am not opposed to alternative parenting methods. There are people, including experts, that swear by experimental or extreme child rearing techniques, but that doesn't mean they all work or are even safe. I am sure that the parent who recently made her child run for hours as a form of punishment thought she was spot on when it came to disciplining her child. The problem is that the child died as a result. In another case a mother made her twelve year old girl wear diapers to school because the child got a few bad grades. I will not even bother to mention the parents that beat their children almost to the point of death because they believe the kids are possessed by the devil.

So what actually is the damage in allowing children well past the infant stage to breast feed? Peer pressure for one thing. Children can be mean and I am certain that the four year old featured on the cover of Time will not be well received by his peers. There is also the issue of what is good for the mother. It has been my experience that while breast feeding may be a good way for a mother and child to bond, once it goes past the infant stage a woman runs the risk of becoming obsessed with their child. Especially male children.

A good example of this is a woman that I know who lives in New York City. She is a relative by marriage and tried to breast feed her son until he was almost six years old. She only stopped trying because his school began to complain that her son mentioned the breast feeding to a teacher and told the educator that he wished his mom would stop. Now an adult, he cannot move out of his mother's house because she says that if he does she will kill herself.

Let's go back to the beginning. Given the recent problems with infant formulas that were outdated or compromised with dangerous ingredients, breast feeding has come back into style in a big way. This has given rebirth to the argument about breast feeding verses formula. The unpopular truth is that not all women should breast feed. Some women experience sore or cracked nipples, embarrassing leakage, the problem of trying to find a place where they can breast feed modestly in public, pass on medications they take to their child, discover their breasts become misshapen, or may over feed without a way to properly measure their child's intake.

Some problems are easily fixed. Special bras and tops make public breast feeding easier and many stores and restaurants now provide private spaces for that purpose. Women who want to breast feed also have the option of using a breast pump to measure out the correct amount of nourishment for their child, avoid scrutiny by using a bottle when feeding in public and spare themselves the pain inflicted by infants that have teeth coming in. However, there is still the problem of proper diet and age. There are studies that show women who give birth after the age of forty are more likely to breast feed their children, but may not be able to pass the correct nutrients on to their kids.

Contrary to recent and highly suspect information about breast feeding, what a mother eats does effect the amount of nutrition their child receives from breast feeding. This is especially true if the mom is a vegetarian or does not have a well balanced diet. That doesn't mean that she cannot breast feed, but it does require the addition of formula or special supplements to the child's diet that are approved by a doctor or licensed nutritionist.

In the end I feel that the Time Magazine cover and the various ads featuring breast feeding moms and their kids are less about the breast feeding debate and more about making sales. However, I am concerned about the amount of false or misleading information that comes along with the hype of provocative photos. Before you make any decision about breast feeding regarding benefits verses problems and how long is too long when it comes to breast feeding past infancy consider this: Breast feeding is NOT a one size fits all issue.

Every woman and child is different. Despite constant attempts to classify body types, the necessary daily intake of vitamins and various foods, and how much is too much, our bodies all beg to differ. Genetics often dictate our body types and the amount of food we need to stay healthy. With that in mind, any woman trying to make a decision about breast feeding should stop reading those pamphlets found in doctor's offices and actually ask the doctor for a recommendation.

Experts disagree on many aspects of breast feeding, that's why the decision you make about breast feeding and all the aspects of it should be yours alone. That decision must be based on established facts, not trendy child nutrition or parenting methods, and should take into consideration the needs and wellbeing of yourself and your child.

Chapter Two: Parenting: Problem Child: A Solution

Several years ago I watched a movie called Problem Child. The film was a comedy about adoptive parents who bring a Charles Manson-like kid into their home. The young boy's Hero is a serial killer and the kid lives up to the motto, "Don't get mad, get even!" It was a comedic version of the Bad Seed film made years before. But unlike the Bad Seed film, this movie featured a boy who could be redeemed. He had problems, but unlike the young girl in the Bad Seed, wasn't some sort of Ted Bundy-like sociopath lacking the conscience to make rational decisions.

Problem Child was a sort of laugh therapy for anyone with children. We've all been through times with our kids when we've been certain they had been implanted in our family by evil space aliens. But I doubt the film was very amusing to those who really do have problem children. For many parents, life is a daily struggle between themselves and their kids. And the problem seems to be growing both in size and severity.

Children are not just misbehaving, but committing very adult crimes. In the last few years we have seen more then a few thirteen and fourteen year olds charged with murder. Kids kill other kids for the fun of it. Teens that aren't allowed to stay out late shoot their parents. Young adults bring guns to school for revenge against teachers and other students. What can be done?

In some cases the answer is as plain as the nose on your face. People have kids, ignore them, let them run wild, shift them from person to person and then are shocked when they lash out and do something really crazy. I recently saw two good examples of this on the news. I live in Phoenix where a five year was found wondering the parking lot of a mall at ten o'clock at night by himself. His home was less then a mile away, but his parent was an alcoholic who often passed out and took no preventative measures to keep her young child fro wandering out the door. Having gone without two meals that day, the child went to a place where he knew food was available. Would anyone be surprised if this child ended up with serious psychological problems?

In another case, a Gilbert, Arizona, Teenager was arrested for plotting a Columbine-style massacre at Gilbert High School. Notes were found indicating a plot to kill teachers and students. The teen had been involved and obsessed with the gothic lifestyle. Her mother often left her with Grandparents. It was obvious that this girl didn't have much of a home life. And that's the key. It's the dreaded, "I've had children, now I actually have to do more work by raising them," scenario. But before I get into dumping on imperfect parents, let's assume that none of us are perfect and most of us have less then ideal situations for raising kids. Under those circumstances, there are still some things that can be done to help out children make it to adulthood without a rap sheet or too many bumps in the road.

Most bad behaviors that children exhibit are in response to their situation. Kids are understanding, but don't understand. A ten year old will say to a friend who wants to come over and play, "I have to stay in by myself until my parents get home and nobody can come over." Personally, I would never leave a ten year old by themselves, but I don't want this to turn into a morality lesson. People sometimes do what they have to do. That ten year old understands the rules, but is going to replace time spent with friends or parents with something else. It might be time online with a stranger who wants to abduct them or time spent with a friendly neighbor who offers to baby sit and wants to molest them. If you don't spend time with your children, someone or something else will.

All children want attention. It's more then just desire, it's hardwired into their brain. They require role models to learn from. They want to watch you, talk with you and understand the things that you do so they can copy your behavior. It's how they become who they are. If a child's role model becomes the TV set, you might have a problem. I limit the number of wild or violent children's programs my kids watch so that they don't end up bouncing off the walls. I don't eliminate those types of programs altogether, because the idea isn't to try and shield your kids from life, it's to teach them how to live it. But bad behavior isn't always the result of too much television or clueless parents.

Unacceptable behavior in children sometimes has little or nothing to do with parents. It can be the result of a number of complicated issues that are out of everyone's control. A few years ago I was an in-studio guest on a radio station in Pennsylvania for the purpose of promoting one of my seminars. The radio personalities encouraged people to phone in their questions, but one young Caller really upset them. During a commercial break, they told me that a young boy, probably ten or eleven years old, called their station every morning to taunt them. He would say disturbing things and sometimes use foul language. This is not a unique situation and the cause may be frustration.

Frustration is a powerful force in children. It's the only outlet they have for situations they feel powerless to control. The child who is frustrated will re-direct that frustration into negative behavior against perceived enemies. A child who is bored because they lack the intelligential stimulation needed for their individual level of intelligence will lash out by exhibiting creative, but also delinquent behavior. The kid who calls a radio station to taunt people does so to get attention and show that he or she can exercise their own kind of power over adults. The child who has become the object of bullying, discrimination or taunting at school may strike back by planning to attack or even kill what they perceive as enemies.

Most children experience three types of frustration, mild, severe and dangerous. Mild frustration is a step above annoyance and can be seen in a child when they refuse to obey or rebel against authority of any kind. Severe frustration is usually the next step up from mild and involves physical violence. In a such a state, a child may hit their parents, a teacher or simply shut down and refuse to do anything regardless of the consequences. Dangerous frustration involves a kid who has become so frustrated that they feel only a desperate act will end their pain. Many children who are dangerously frustrated got there without the other two steps. Under constant pressure from all directions, they simply decide to strike back. Remember, most adolescents and teens don't look at adults as people who can or would help them. They are unlikely to call a help line or ask anyone at home or school for assistance.

There are several ways that parents can fight frustration in their children:

1. Understand your child's mental state. If a child seems moody, try and find out what's bothering them. Ask about their day at school. Keep track of their activities and reinforce the fact that you are able to help them with problems they might think are beyond your expertise or grasp. When you discover a problem in their life, try your best to solve it.

2. Don't antagonize your child. We see it all the time. Parents under pressure or with their own set of issues say NO to kids just for the sake of saying NO. And they say it with undue severity. If you get a rise or some authoritarian high out of bossing your kids around, it might be a good idea to place them in foster care and buy some dogs. Then you're only problems with be with the animal rights folks.

3. Don't be the cause of their frustration. Parents involved in constant on-going conflicts like a divorce, remarriage or custody arguments create a lot of problems for their kids. If your plan is get back or revenge, the biggest victims are likely to be your children.

4. Follow Through with Behavior Correction. If you say they'll get time out, make sure they do. Always follow through.

Chapter Three: Parenting: When The Kids Won't Listen

Are you about to drive a nail into your head? Have the kiddies made you so crazy that you've asked your partner to smack you right between the eyes with a baseball bat? Hey, with seven children of my own, I have been there! Before you loose what's left of your sanity, let me offer a few suggestions.

Whether you have one child or many, they can make your life a living nightmare if you don't get to the root cause of the problem and lay down some ground rules for the household. Let's start by looking at what the problem isn't. The kids aren't being jerks because you are married, single, divorced or remarried. Despite what many so called experts tell you, most children develop their own agenda based on their own needs.

Trying to reason with children is ridiculous and comes from the failed theory that we, as parents, have let them down in some way. If you find yourself in a situation that may be less then desirable for your child, explain it to them. This might be a need to move, divorce, remarriage or the presence of a step parent. Let your child know that you love them and really care about them, but never apologize for your family situation. Never tell kids, "Dad and I are getting a divorce, but we want you to know that it's not your fault." Just the use of the word 'fault' and the inclusion of the child in the process, immediately has the opposite affect intended. Make sure that you explain any new or expected change to your family situation to your child or children as far in advance as possible. This fosters trust and helps reassure them.

Children should never be made to feel guilty for whatever situation the family finds itself in. Most kids act out because parents knowingly or unknowingly place guilt on them. Why? Because kids aren't emotionally prepared or able to deal with guilt. Making children feel bad for no reason is a losing situation. That doesn't mean that they shouldn't be held responsible for bad acts. If your child does something that injures another, destroys or does damage to your home, endangers their own welfare or shows severe disrespect for an adult, there should be consequences. Those consequences should always include a specific punishment that lasts for a specific period of time.

My older son had a bad habit of not checking in with me and staying out past whatever time I told him to be home. Given the problem of child abductions, I always insist on knowing where my kids are and limit their ability to be anywhere by themselves. When he was eleven years old, my son went over to play with a friend on a Saturday morning. I knew where he was and had the phone number to his friend's house. But when my son hadn't checked in with us by four o'clock in the afternoon, I called his friend only to find that he had left hours before. Given that, my wife and I set out to find him and spent the next several hours frantically looking for him.

Finally, just as we were about to involve the Police, my son walked in the door at nearly eight thirty in the evening. He explained how that he had joined in with another group of friends to play some football and lost track of time. That incident upset the entire family and, needless to say, could have ended very differently. As a result, I grounded my son for three months. Why so harsh? Because he had been late before and I knew that he was putting his own life and well being in jeopardy by engaging in this sort of behavior. He learned his lesson and never failed to check in with me after that. Most missing kids are missing either because their parents allowed them to freely roam the streets or they failed to listen to their parents and be where they were supposed to be. Setting limits can avoid tragedy.

The biggest need most kids have is for a portion of your time. Not giving it to them is a certain recipe for bad behavior. If you will not give them your time and attention, they will do something bad to get it. Once you allow some time for a child, see what interests them the most. Some children are readers, others like to draw and all like to play. Being a Speaker, I have spent a lot of time on the road. When I was home, I made sure to involve my kids in everything I did. I bought a huge bin of play blocks and placed it in my home office for my younger children. They were always welcome to come in and play while I worked. I encouraged my older kids to answer the phone and help send faxes. Sure, it made things a bit harder for me, but I knew it was the right thing to do.

The greatest problem that parents face today is deciding how much they love their children. Sound strange? Loving your kids means having to give up a certain things in favor of raising happy and healthy individuals. If you love yourself more then your kids, get ready for a rough ride. I have met more then just a few parents who hand their kids a key to the house, order a pizza, throw them a c-note and head out for a skiing weekend. Others move from relationship to relationship with absolutely no interest in how it may affect their children. Loving your kids doesn't mean having to give up everything, never going out or having no love life. But it does require that you provide them with as stable an environment as possible and take them into consideration when you make personal or family decisions.

Stability means responsibility. Allowing children to be by themselves for extended periods of time is a formula for disaster. While it might seem fun to them at first, most will grow to resent it and try and get back at you by getting in trouble. If you're the kind of parent that still acts as though they had no children or are reliving your teen years, don't bother wondering why your kids have problems. Refusing to be a responsible parent has nothing to do with being married, single, divorced, separated or remarried. Those are your choices and you have the right to make them. What it does mean is that you will be there when they need you, dispense reasonable punishment when it's required and make time for them. If both parents are present in the home, they should always present a united front when dealing with their children. Problems begin when parents fight in front of the kids, disagree with each other on privileges for them or allow unacceptable behavior to go unpunished.

If you have problem kids or kid problems, it may be because you do not spell out what household opportunities are privileges to be earned, and which are merely a part of living in the home. In our house privileges are watching TV or videos, going on the computer, being allowed outside to play and being taken out to the movies, a restaurant, the library or other entertainment. Houses Rules include no fighting, mutual respect, chores to be done and obeying parents. If the rules get broken, privileges are cut back or discontinued for a period of time. We help our kids to learn responsibility by assigning chores and never asking them to do anything we haven't done or aren't willing to do ourselves. When it's time to clean the house, we all chip in and get the job done.

It's disturbing to see children who are allowed to run wild with no expectation of responsibility from them. Irresponsible kids often have irresponsible parents. Part of being responsible means teaching kids to be good neighbors and being a good neighbor yourself. I am glad that my kids go up to the neighbors and offer to help when furniture needs to be moved, a dog is lost and needs to found or when a babysitter is needed. This doesn't mean that I haven't had to break up free for alls when the kids go at it! Nobody's perfect and any parent can expect their fair share of trouble when it comes to dealing with children.

Chapter Four: Parenting: Children Without Hope: The Cause Of and Cure For Suicides Among Young People

Suicides in our society are on the rise. Even the U.S. Military is concerned because they have seen suicide rates in their ranks skyrocket over the past few decades. Especially tragic is the ever-increasing number of suicides among adolescents and teens. Scarcely a week goes by that I do not hear about a child or teen taking their own life or making an attempt to do so.

The primary causes of suicide will always be debatable. You really can't look into the mind of some other person to find out why they decided to end their life and their reason for doing so might be very personal. Experts tell us that some of the off the shelf causes for suicide can be mental illness, stress, drug and alcohol abuse, bullying or just feeling left out and alone. However, I think it really all comes down to having a sense of hopelessness. This is especially true among young people because they lack the maturity or life skills to cope with those kinds of feelings for very long.

Whether we like it or not, society has to take some responsibility for the high rate of suicide among young people. It is any wonder that children feel a sense of hopelessness when all they see is a constant flow of negative reports and dire economic, social and environmental predictions in the news, and prophet of doom style commentaries from political pundits, on all types of media? The old saying "garbage in, garbage out" certain applies to this situation.

The one place that should be a safe haven for young people often becomes the instrument of torture that leads them to desperate acts. Schools have become a micro-chasm of all of society's ills. Kids experience harassment, bullying and can become social outcasts within their own peer group just because of the way they look, speak or the clothes they wear. Then there is the hyper-negativism: Students are constantly taught about and reminded of our planet's environmental and social ills by lesson plans that seem more interested in soothing the consciences of adults, than teaching the basics to children.

Young people have enough to deal with when it comes to just growing up. We do not need to constantly flood their minds with issues that will likely never be solved. Parents can help counteract what happens in school by being vigilant at home. This begins with monitoring what their kids watch, who they listen to and what is being said about them on social media web-sites and their own cell phones. It's a lot of work, but I am sure that parents who have already lost children to hopelessness would gladly go back and do all these things if they had a second chance.

Parents also need to be sure that their kids are being exposed to positive role models and activities that promote physical and mental wellness. Part of this process means always keeping the lines of communication open between parents and their children. If you know what your child likes, you can find and suggest activities for him or her that will maintain their interest and inspire them. You can also avoid getting them involved with activities they don't really care about, avoiding the risk of further alienating them from you.

Adolescents and teens love to dig deep down inside themselves for introspection, socialize with their own peer group (for the most part) and avoid communication with their parents at all costs. Parents have to find ways to break down those walls. One way is to not build any additional ones. Make time for your kids when they do want to talk. Give them your full attention (turn off the TV, radio, computer, etc.). Look for opportunities to socialize with them apart from the role of parenting. This doesn't mean being a friend instead of being a parent. It just means that there are times when you should create opportunities for communication by sharing an activity (movies, TV shows, sporting events, live theater, whatever!) you both have interest in. This opens the door for honest discussion and conversational exchanges.

I have always supported the learning process and the underpaid educators involved with it. However, I believe that many schools have simply become failure farms, despite the efforts of sincere educators to keep that from happening. Part of the problem is that political correctness has replaced the basics when it comes to learning. Children do not need to constantly be reminded about all the social ills out there. They get enough of that through just about every media source available, twenty-four/seven. Educators must re-evaluate their lesson plans and begin to replace the negative with the positive.

Another weapon in the fight against adolescent and teen suicide is teaching, legislating and practicing Peer Responsibility. If a young person decides to make someone else the target of insults or bully them because they think it's funny or have problems of their own, they need to know that there will be consequences. These consequences should come before things get so bad that the person being insulted or bullied decides to end their life. Schools must adopt a zero tolerance policy when it comes to harassing and bullying and really enforce it. Students must be made aware that these practices will not be tolerated and those that fail to report them will be subject to the same punishment as those who carry out these harmful activities.

Now I'm sure that I will not make any friends with this next suggestion to help stop suicides among young people: I believe it's time for schools, institutions and businesses involved with the education or treatment of young people to extend the welcome mat to the diety that made all life possible in the first place. I'm talking about God. You can call him a "higher power" or "the man upstairs" or "the power in charge" if you like. That's how some in twelve step programs refer to him and that's fine for them and society as a whole. I call him God and believe it's time to show him the respect he deserves. If we respect and trust in the one who made us, we'll have the faith to confront and over-come our problems. We'll also respect ourselves enough to avoid sur-coming to life's struggles by committing suicide.

God has not been welcome in schools for a long time. Even when he was, most 'modern' educators re-framed from teaching much, if anything, about him unless it was historically, socially or scientifically relevant. Well folks, times they are a-changing again. It's time to let young people know that there is a higher power out there and that he cares about them. I'm not saying that we should force God down anyone's throat. I am saying that schools should allow groups of students to meet, pray and study whatever holy book they lean towards at least once during the school day if they care to. Teachers that believe in God should be able to allow students to decide if they want to opt in to classes about God, religions or religious beliefs.

There is no guarantee that such changes in the public school system would prevent or stop all suicides. There is, however, a chance that instilling the kind of moral and ethical values that most religions teach would help to close the flood gates of harassing, bullying and suicides that now seem wide open. Most suicides among young people occur in public (non-religious) schools, not in schools where the concept of God and/or religion is welcome and taught openly. As a Christian, I wake up each day and am filled with hope despite all that happens in the world around me. Imagine if most kids could feel the same way.

Chapter Five: Parenting: Create An Action Plan To Combat Negative Behavior

In many homes around America the best way to describe the relationship between children and their parents is ALL OUT WAR! It's reminiscent of the trench warfare so common during World War I. Both sides are dug in and everyone lives each day in a perpetual stalemate. If that's you, there is a way out. You have to create an Action Plan that will get both you and your children out of the trenches and into the peace talks.

Wars that are won by all out aggression tend to exact a heavy toll on both sides. In some instances, a war can be won or some sort of truce can be reached by talking with the enemy, looking at the root causes of the war and deciding on compromises that will satisfy both sides. The same is true of volatile family situations where parents and children are constantly butting heads on just about everything.

Action Plans are all about change. The first thing that needs to change is that you and your kids must stop looking at each other as the enemy. The best way to alter those perceptions is by ending the BLAME GAME. That means putting the past behind you and working towards a future where you respect one another. This happens when parents and children understand, to the best of their abilities, each other's roles, duties and responsibilities in a household.

Conversation will be difficult, but it's essential. Begin by talking out each other's perception of the roles you play in the family dynamic. Let your kids explain to you what they believe your responsibilities are. You tell them what you believe is expected of them. Examine the problems or failures on both sides without blaming and always avoid labels. For example, do not tell your child, "It's your job to do the dishes. You don't do them because your lazy." Stick to the issue. The dishes are NOT getting done by the person chosen to do them and THAT is the problem, nothing more.

EXPLAIN instead of BLAME. Tell your child that if he or she doesn't do the dishes, someone else has to and that is not fair. Explain to them that the same thing would be true if you asked your child to get a job, go out and work and pay bills that you should be paying. Everyone has their place in a family and all must contribute to the success of the family dynamic by playing the part best suited to them. You should also be sure that your child understands the correct ways to accomplish the chores you assign to them.

Sometimes problem solving means simply making a job easier. When it comes to dishes, they should be scraped and soaked as soon as possible. Most kids probably don't know that soaking dishes in a sink will make them easier to do after a short period of time. Instead, many will stand at the sink and try to scrap off food particles that are caked on, making the chore nothing more than a lesson in frustration. If you have a dish washer, the dishes should be scraped and placed in the washer as soon after dinner as practical. Again, it's about making chores easier by making sure that the kids know the proper way to accomplish the tasks that you assign to them.

Secondary to talking things out with the kids, parents have to work on their Action Plan apart from interaction with their children. Once you get past the blame issues, make a list of all the problem behaviors that occur in your household and in include your own, if applicable. Think about what you can do to make sure your children have full confidence in you as a parent. Then, think about what they can do to restore your faith and confidence in them. The key to success is making sure that you maintain your parental authority without making your children feel that Authority means Bullying. The kids must understand that your job is to keep them safe and make sure they grow up equipped with the skills needed to face everyday life.

When it comes to your Action Plan, stick to the basics. What are the MAIN problem areas or negative behaviors in the house? How often do these behaviors occur and what sets them off? What has worked and what hasn't worked to alter these behaviors? Most importantly, what EXACTLY is it that you want your children to do and what do you believe they expect of you in terms of positive changes? These are important matters to think about before you sit down and discuss problems in the home further with your kids.

The next time you speak with your children make sure there are few, if any, interruptions. Be certain that they are listening to what you have to say and that you are listening to them. Hearing and really listening are two separate things. If the kids feel that the purpose of your meeting with them is to merely deliver an ultimatum instead of talking things out and respectively listening to each other's viewpoints, the whole thing is pointless. Open communication and active listening allow for this process to go forward in a positive way.

Identify and list the things that you and your children believe need to change in your home. Discuss ways to solve these problems. Alternative choices are a good start. This means replacing behaviors that cause trouble with those that do not and are agreeable to both sides. If children feel they are saddled with too many chores, consider splitting the chores up among everyone in the home. Children might have to take on some of your chores according to their abilities so that they understand the concept of fairly working together for the common good.

When chores are not done or negative behaviors remain unaltered, there must be consequences for the offending parties. Consequences should be realistic, enforcable and consistent. Do not threaten punishment unless you are absolutely willing to IMMEDIATELY carry it out! If you keep telling a child that you will place them in Time-Out if they do not do their homework, you have to follow through. If you do not, your child will know that the consequences you assign are really just empty threats that you probably will not carry out.

Apart from following through on consequences for inaction or negative behaviors, the second most important thing in your Action Plan is that everyone in your family understands WHY certain behaviors MUST be expected of them. They do not necessarily have to agree with them. There are times when parents have to lay down the law in order to establish and maintain a peaceful environment where everyone in the home works together and understands their place in the family dynamic.

Parents should never give up the authority they have to the whims of their children. Children must not be allowed to rule the house. However, if parents show weakness and an inability to be fair with their kids and constantly berate or badger them, anarchy will likely be the result. Parents must listen attentively to their children, consider all sides of an issue, retain their authority, work for a more peaceful and productive atmosphere in the home and always follow through on any consequences they assign.

Chapter Six: Parenting: The Power Of Positive Parenting

We live in a world that constantly reminds us about the NEGATIVES in life. It's tough to get through even one hour a day without some media prophet of doom, nay sayer or pundit reminding us about how bad things are. It is any wonder that most of us have negative self thoughts? These thoughts quickly become actions and get passed on to others, including our families.

Negativity is not something that most people willingly accept. We are naturally turned off by negative people, things and ideas. It's forced on us by those already indoctrinated into its insidious attributes. These include sadness, hopelessness and surrender to a culture that thrives on bad news. Conversely, positive people tend to be infectious and spread optimism to all those they meet throughout the day.

The people in our lives who are most vulnerable to Negativity are children. Young children, adolescents and even most teens lack the emotional, social and behavioral skills to process and deal with a constant flow of negative information and actions. It's bad enough that many face things like bullying at school, but when parents join in by labeling their kids or failing to recognize negative self imagining, things go from bad to worse.

What we say today can affect a child for their entire life. That's why parents have to be careful not to label their children by making these kinds of statements:

"You're too stupid to understand why I am telling you to do this; but you had better do it anyway."

"You're a real slob. Only a slob would make a mess like this!"

"I was never as lazy as you are. You had better get your act together."

Parents also need to watch for statements made by their kids that may indicate serious self-esteem issues caused by themselves or others:

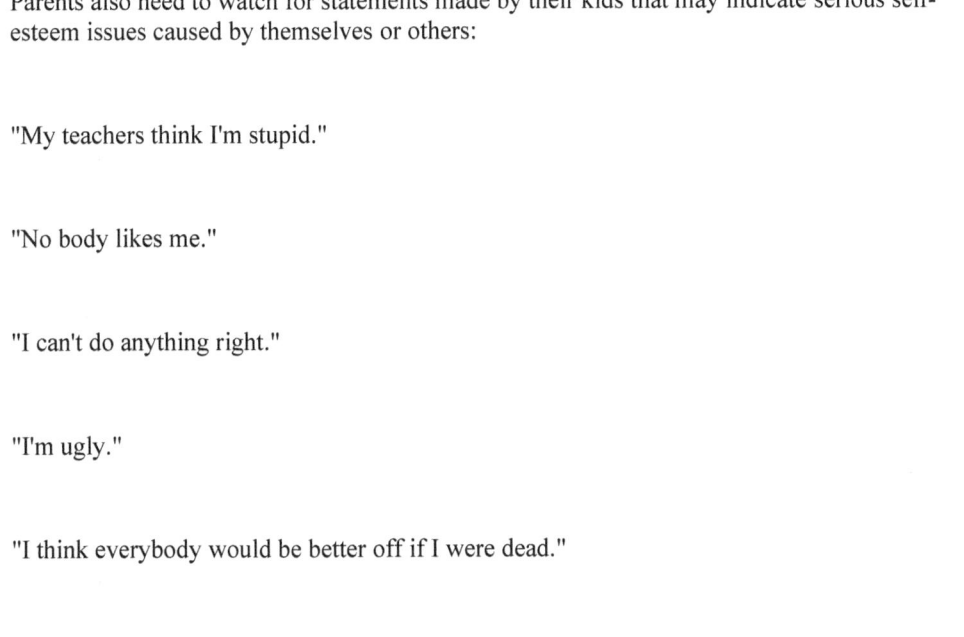

"My teachers think I'm stupid."

"No body likes me."

"I can't do anything right."

"I'm ugly."

"I think everybody would be better off if I were dead."

These kinds of ideas do not just fly into a child's brain. They are planted there by others: Family, friends, teachers, authority figures. If your child is saying these kinds of things, you need to find out why and take positive actions to change his or her self evaluation. If not, disaster can follow in the form of self-destructive behavior. Some kids will lash out verbally or physically. Others will cut themselves, hurt themselves, try to hurt others, break the law or attempt suicide.

Start your positive parenting program by getting to the source of any ideas that may be causing your child or children to have low self esteem. Make sure you are not a part of the problem. Think carefully about the things you say to them. Set house rules so that RESPECT replaces verbal or physical abuse by siblings. Make sure influences outside of the home are not causing or adding to them problem. Speak to teachers and other authority figures in your child's life and talk to their friends.

Sometimes speaking to your child's friends and even their classmates can yield information that you might not be able to get from teachers or authority figures who may not recognize the problems or may even be a part of them. Bullies are easy to spot because they don't tend to think that what they are doing is wrong; they might even think it's funny. A bully may say something like this to you: "So, you are that Nerd's Mom!" I have seen this happen.

Once you get things cleaned up outside the home and make it clear to everyone in the family that negativity, bullying or verbal and physical abuse if not an option, start working on your child's self esteem. Ask them to make a list of positive personal attributes. Concentrate on the positive things that they and others would notice about their body, personality, skills and talents. Encourage them to begin a daily diary or journal of thoughts and things in their life that they are willing to share with you at the end of every week.

Dairies will include what is important in a child's life. Knowing what is important to them can help you be a better parent. This is especially true if you find more negative statements than positive ones on a regular basis. This gives you a starting point to work out those kinds of things with your child. Remember, they probably do not possess the intellectual tools to cope with constant negativity. You have to try and replace as much of that negativity as you can and help them to learn how to cope and deal with whatever remains.

It can be a benefit to your child and you to try and bring positive things and people into your lives. Take them to see an uplifting movie. Attend religious services at a church that has a track record of turning kids on to positive things and ideas. Suggest books and media that entertain, but also inspire them. Watch out for obsessions that your child might have with negative people, ideas, video games, books, television or on line programming. Replace these with positive things.

Be sure that you acknowledge positive behavior. If your child gets a good grade, finishes a chore on time or does something else that deserves notice, make sure you thank them and tell them how much you appreciate the positive things they do everyday. Rewards are also good, but should not be excessive. Sometimes just taking your child shopping with you, to a favorite park or event is enough to let them know that they are on the right path and that you appreciate them.

No child's life is going to be perfect and no parent is going to be able to raise a perfect child. What we all can do is to make sure that our attention is constantly focused on the lives of our children. This allows us to be proactive and see problems coming before our kids are so overwhelmed by them that they give up and give in to despair.

Chapter Seven: Parental Survival Skills: Getting Your Children and Teens to Listen and Obey

There are no easy answers when it comes to deciding how to communicate or deal with with your children in a manner that will get them to change problem behavior. The best way is to start with a simple goal like getting them to listen to you and respond in a positive way. Easier said than done? Maybe, but let me show you some proven and effective ways to get your point across and change your children's bad behavior patterns without having to bang your head against the wall.

Plan to succeed by deciding what it is you want to communicate to your children, what discipline methods will work best with them and how you can help them to avoid problem behavior in the first place. Start by keeping your communications with them simple. Don't lecture or tell them what happened when you were a kid. Say what you mean and mean what you say. Keep your sentences short, speak clearly and always remain calm.

Children learn from their parents. If you yell and fly off the handle, so will they. If you hit and beat them (which you should never do), they will learn that violence is a way to try and get people to do what you want them to do. If you warn them not to do something and offer a punishment if they do not obey, make sure that you follow through. Otherwise, your kids will learn that all your threats are empty ones and just keep doing what you do not want them to do.

Do you constantly criticize and never praise your children? Criticism has its place as long as it is carefully worded and constructive. Let's use a messy room situation as an example. If you tell your child, "You are the biggest slob I have ever met," what is that telling them? The answer is: nothing. No only have you insulted your kid, but they still have not actually received any instructions from you. Try this instead: "Clean up your room today. If you do, you will have more room to play and space for your friends when they come over."

That tells a child that's there is something in it for them to clean up. When your child cleans things up or does a chore on time, offer some unexpected praise by thanking them for doing so. If they do not follow your directions to clean the room after at least two warnings, lower the boom with a reasonable punishment. Ground them, give them time-out, refuse to allow their friends to play with them or do all three until their room is cleaned up to your satisfaction.

If you have house rules, make sure your child understands them. Too many parents continually shout out all kinds of demands at their children without telling them exactly what they would like their kids to do. If a child stays outside too long after dark would it be better to say, "Do you think you can stay out all night?" or "You know the rules: Be in before dark." The answer is obvious. Rules remove excuses and replace vague criticisms and insults.

One way to take the sting out of rules is by offering your child some choices. There are kids that would rather sweep the porch than do the dishes or clean the garage instead of taking out the garbage. By offering choices and letting your child decide, you remove yet another reason for them not to do their chores. If they fail to do them, take immediate action. Never put punishments or the assignment of punishment off for more than a short time. If you do, the child will probably not even recall what they did wrong by the time they are punished and will not learn from the punishment.

Children are not perfect and deserve a chance. The last thing you want is to be perceived as an unfair dictator. Most experts recommend that you give kids three chances to complete a task, do a chore or instantly change a negative behavior. If you want a child to stop banging a toy against the wall, ask them to stop. If they do not, tell them to stop. If that fails, take the toy away and give them a suitable punishment like time out or extra chores.

If you want your kids to listen to you, you have to listen to them. If your child wants to talk with you, give them the attention that they deserve. Turn off the TV, move away from the computer and stop text messaging. Listen to them and respond to what they say in an honest and concerned manner. Offer sound advice and do not placate kids by saying that they will feel better in the morning or tell them to get their minds off their troubles. If you do not help your kids with their problems, they will look elsewhere for answers and you do not want them doing that. Try to get to the heart of their problem and help them solve it.

Never use name-calling or labeling in your communications with your kids, Do not tell them they are stupid, dumb, lazy, crazy, act like a baby or make statements like, "You are just like your no-good Uncle Henry." You also do not want to go too far in the other direction by using politically correct psycho-babble responses like, "I see... That makes sense... I understand... Really... How about that...I feel your pain" and so on. Be kind, be fair, be honest and be yourself.

Children like reinforcement. Sometimes that want to talk to you about a very simply problem to see if you are willing to invest the time and effort required to help them solve it. For example: Your child says, "All my friends are away for the weekend and I have nothing to do." Ask them if they would like to do something with you. Perhaps you both could go to the park, visit the local library, see a movie, throw a baseball around or do something else you often do together. You can also suggest they go out and try to make some new friends in the neighborhood or visit a neighbor's child that they have not spoken to in a while.

You should never play Let's Make A Deal with your kids. If you do it once, they will expect it again. Do not compromise your authority or their safety. There are going to be plenty of times when you will have to stand your ground, especially with teens. Things like dating, wearing make-up, inappropriate physical relationships, staying out late at night, failing courses at school or driving a friends car without your permission (or perhaps even a driver's license) are good examples.

Teens have reached a stage of development that is preparing them for life on their own. This makes is difficult to keep them in line with house rules designed to rein in their desire to be completely independent before they are ready and to protect them from harm. Teens believe they will live forever and many think they know everything, so any arguments deigned to appeal to common sense or warn against the possible dire consequences of their actions will likely fail.

Teens want respect and freedom, but those things have to be earned. Let them no that. Make a short but comprehensive list of rules you need for them to follow. Each time they break a rule, there must be an instant consequence. Teens love to communicate, so taking away phone or computer privileges for a reasonable period of time is a good start. If they stay out late, ground them. If they still try and go out or habitually break the rule about staying out late, take away their I.D. and place a pad lock on their closet so that they do not have instant access to clothes except for sweats or pajamas to wear around the house.

You have to protect your kids because they probably will place what they believe is having fun above protecting themselves. If you feel your kids might be experimenting with drugs, have them drug-tested during a scheduled doctor's office appointment. If they are using drugs, take immediate steps to stop that behavior. Keep them away from the drugs and the drugs away from them. This could mean no longer allowing them out of the house on their own. It might also mean placing them in a stricter educational environment (by changing schools or home schooling). Regular and unexpected drug tests should also be performed to be sure they are following the rules.

Inappropriate physical relationships are a huge problem among teens and always have been. Teens do not understand the long range and very serious consequences that can arise from what they consider to be just "fooling around." There are no easy ways to deal with these except to limit the times that teens have alone with their peers. Grounding and isolation from other kids has to be handled delicately to avoid making your teen a social outcast. This should be a last resort, not a first response if you suspect your teen is having that type of a physical relationship.

The most important consideration in any step you take must always be the health and safety of your child. Before you lower the boom with a complete grounding and total isolation, try to give your teen some wiggle room by allowing them out within strictly set parameters. Make it a rule that at no time are they to be alone with a known or perceived girl or boy friend. This rule should extend to the point that your teen is not allowed to be anywhere that might offer them the opportunity to be completely un-supervised by responsible adults.

Check up on your teen and make sure they check in with you on an hourly basis when they are out on their own. Make this a hard and fast rule that has instant consequences if broken. If you allow them to take charge of and run their own life, they will probably run it right into the ground. Remember, it's not only in your child's best interests to keep them out of trouble, it is in yours as well. There are many jurisdictions where parents are now held equally responsible for the actions of their children. Parents are being fined or even jailed when their adolescent or teen children get out of control and habitually break the law.

There are no shortcuts to good parenting. You have to be positive, decisive, proactive and responsible when it comes to your children. You must be a good listener, constant companion, fair judge and always follow through with any reasonable punishment when children and teens refuse to behave, break the house rules or decide to test the limits of how often you will exert your authority.

Chapter Eight: Parenting: Six Huge Parenting Mistakes

Parents are not perfect and no one has all the answers when it comes to raising children. What we can do is make sure that the methods we use to raise up our children are positive, proven and productive. The best way to be sure we accomplish this is by recognizing methods that are adversarial, antagonistic and arbitrary. Many parents use these kinds of methods because they were used on them as children. That brings us to our first huge parenting mistake...

1. Passing abuse and negative parenting methods on to your children.

Children learn by observation and tend to copy the behavior of their parents when they become adults. If a child was injured or traumatized by his or her parents, they may do the same or something similar as adults to their children because it is the parenting method that was used on them. If regular and severe beatings or some other form of physical abuse was involved, they might reinterpret that behavior and repeat it in a different form such as verbal abuse.

It is important to recognize that our parents may have made mistakes in the way they raised us and replace whatever negative parenting methods they used with positive ones. Equally important is the need to make sure we are not simply trading one form of abuse for another. Verbal abuse can be as damaging in almost as many ways as physical abuse. That brings us to our next huge parenting mistake...

2. Screaming at and threatening your children.

The only message you send to your kids when you scream at them is that you are unstable and they are worthless. You are not actually explaining anything to them, just venting your own feelings and frustrations. When you are hostile toward them or make threats like "Now you're gonna get it!" you are telling your kids that violence is the way to deal with anything they do wrong. Whether it is failing to obey a command or accidently spilling a cup of milk on the dinner table, kids that are screamed at and threatened will instantly go into a mood of fear and dread that can only harm their personality development and sense of self worth.

Children cannot learn anything positive from those kinds of experiences. They will tend to live in fear and never learn to fully trust parents that scream at or threaten them. Children that do learn to obey based on fear are children that end up believing that hostility is the best way to solve problems or to get your point across. They tend to be more rebellious and develop an abnormal view of personal relationships. Hostility directed at them also causes children to replace their love or respect for their parents with fear. That kind of emotional redirection may well come back to haunt parents that yell and threaten when kids are old enough and strong enough to strike back at them.

3. Constantly questioning your children.

When you ask your child something like "Why can't you just listen to me and behave yourself?" you are displaying a lack of the ability to manage their behavior. You should be pointing out exactly what they are doing wrong, telling them what you need for them to do to correct it and provide them with a reasonable amount of time to carry out your request. Children do not need negative statements disguised as questions, they need answers and positive parenting.

4. Begging your children to behave.

Begging or pleading with children to do what you want them to do accomplishes nothing. It sends a message to children and that message is that you are not in control and do not know how to be in control. Begging passes your authority over to them and places your kids in charge. If you prefer to be in charge, do not plead with children to behave. Make them understand in a positive and affirming way that proper behavior is not an option and that bad behavior cannot and will not be tolerated. Be sure they understand exactly what you want them to do. Have simple and easy to understand house rules so that they always know what they can and cannot do.

5. Lecturing your children about anything and everything.

"I never disobeyed my parents the way you disobey me when I was a child!" It sounds like a logical argument, but not to kids. They were not there when you were a child and could not experience whatever you did as a child. Children tune out lectures and learn nothing from them. Replace lecturing or speech-making with direct, assertive statements that tell a child exactly what you expect of them, when you expect it and what the consequences will be if they fail to obey you.

6. Allowing others to be substitute parents.

Proper parenting means learning from our mistakes and looking for positive ways to nurture and mentor our kids. If we do not do these things, children will turn to others for the love, support and direction that they crave. These 'others' might be friends, relatives or neighbors that may not have their best interests in mind. Child predators, for example, look for opportunities with children who have parents that are unable or unwilling to properly supervise or watch their kids.

Chapter Nine: Parenting: To Spank or Not To Spank: That Is The Question

Like most parents I struggled with the dilemma of spanking when my first child came along. I read a lot of material on the subject and even took parenting classes along with my wife. Both of us were motivated by a desire to do what was best for our child. After all that, we were still split between the two schools of thought concerning punishment for children. Should I spank or not? The answer did not come easy and my wife and I decided it should be a personal decision for both of us.

I considered a lot of things in making my decision. On the one side, there are those who say that spanking is a temporary and unsatisfactory measure to alter a child's behavior that seriously affects their self-esteem and personal growth. On the other side, there were the traditional and religious arguments that say things like 'spare the rod and spoil the child.' More than a few people from the spanking side of the argument believe that any parent who doesn't spank is a coward that is going against the natural order of things. They claim spanking helps to break a child's will and make him or her more obedient.

There were always stories in the media about extreme cases of spanking or corporal punishment that caused a child to be injured or even killed. In almost every case the parents were obsessed with the notion that there kids were bad, evil or just naturally disobedient. I couldn't see myself or my wife ever taking spanking to that kind of a physical extreme, but hearing about those incidents brought to mind my own childhood experiences of being spanked.

I have been told that it is unwise to use your own youthful trials and tribulations as a consideration or deciding factor in how you will parent and raise your children. Despite that unwritten rule, I couldn't help but recall what spanking meant to me. It didn't happen very often, but I did get spanked a few times and those experiences were memorable. The first spanking I can remember happened when I was in first grade. We had a substitute teacher on one occasion that, for whatever reason, truly hated me.

The teacher kept calling out my name all day. She said I was talking or doing something else wrong and that just wasn't true. In fact, I was the quiet kid who barely spoke a word all day and never got in trouble with anyone. Despite my objections, she called my mother on the phone and reported her version of my evil behavior during that school day. My mother believed her and decided to correct my actions with a spanking.

When I got home, she made me drop my pants down to my bare bottom. After I bent over a bench, she proceeded to spank me in a very painful way that brought me to tears. I remember that incident like it happened yesterday. It did not cause me to have low self-esteem because I didn't do anything to deserve the spanking. It did cause me great physical and emotional pain, and much embarrassment. I had no brothers or sisters and was very shy. I did not like removing my clothes for anyone, including my parents.

My mother was in no mood to listen to my side of the story, but I decided that she needed to hear it anyway. After I told her my version of things, she dragged me up to the school to see if the substitute was still there. My mother made it clear that if I was lying, another spanking was coming in my immediate future.

The substitute was still in my classroom finishing up some paper work when my mother and I walked in. She smiled and put on a real show for my mom. She stuck to her story about my behavior and was as convincing a liar as I have ever met anytime in my life. As we walked out of the classroom door, I could already feel the fear of the pain and embarrassment that my next spanking would bring. Instead, God delivered an angel to rescue me in the form of a classmate named Maureen.

Maureen was quiet and I always thought that she was a lot like me. On the day of the spanking incident she just happened to be sitting near the entrance to the school with her mother. They were waiting for someone to pick them up. As I passed by Maureen, she could see that I was upset. I was really surprised when she spoke up and asked if I was alright. Once my mother realized she was a classmate of mine, we stopped briefly so that my mom, Maureen and her mom could exchange greetings. During those brief moments I told my classmate what happened.

Maureen was stunned and told my mother that I never talked in class and confirmed that the substitute had been on my case all day. My mother looked surprised, but she saw the honesty in my classmate's account of what really happened that day and believed her. I knew my mother well enough to know that no apologie was going to be coming my way. I was just happy to have avoided another spanking. She did call the school the next day to file a complaint against the substitute. It didn't do any good, but my regular teacher was upset when she heard about the whole adventure and that substitute was never used for her class again.

I can attest to the fact that my spanking experience was traumatic and left me with the inability to trust anyone, including my mother. I was not better off for it in any way, shape or form. After considering all the information that I have read and my own experiences, I decided that I would not spank my children. My wife came to the same conclusion on her own. I still believe that the decision to spank or not is a personal one that should always be at the discretion of the parent or parents. My children have grown into responsible adults and I couldn't be happier about the way they have turned out and they did it without being spanked.

Chapter Ten: Parenting: Humiliation: Punishment or Persecution?

A dad shoots his daughter's laptop on YouTube because she posted nasty comments about him. A mom takes charge of her daughter's Facebook account, tells her friends that she has been silenced and demands she tell them why if they ask. A grandmother makes her grandson stand at a busy intersection near their home with a sign that says he always disobeys her. A judge orders a man who stole money to walk the streets of his town every weekend for six years wearing a sign that tells the world he's a thief. Is humiliation really the one size fits all solution to correcting bad or unacceptable behavior?

Parents and judges have discovered humiliation as a form of punishment and correction. Some of those that make use of this method argue that they are left with few choices. In the wake of years of an 'out with the old and in with the new' movement against traditional punishments that many feel do not work or are too damaging in the long run, those who have the responsibility to correct bad or irresponsible behavior in others are resorting to what they say are new and creative techniques like outright humiliation.

First of all, humiliation punishment is not anything new. There was a time when public and private school students who did not perform up to the teacher's expectations had to wear a 'dunce cap' in class. The cap looked a bit like a traffic cone or cardinal's headdress and the word 'dunce' meant someone who was incapable of learning. The term was also once a degrading slang word for someone who was 'slow witted' or mentally handicapped. The dunce cap practice went out of style in the early part of the twentieth century.

Another popular form of humiliation punishment was having people suspected of deviant behavior or convicted of minor crimes placed in public stocks. These were typically pieces of wood that somewhat resembled yokes used on oxen with cut outs designed to immobilize the head and hands of the malefactor locked into them. The stocks were placed in public markets or at the center of town, wherever the maximum number of people could see them. The use of stocks began in medieval times, were popular as a punishment in Europe and colonial America until the middle to late 1800s, and may still be in use in some parts of Latin America today.

While there is little doubt that the dunce cap made under-performing students think twice before failing a test or that the use of stocks kept Peeping Toms from peeping, these humiliation punishments also did a lot of unintended damage to innocent victims. Imagine using the dunce cap on someone just because they had a learning disability or placing a mentally disabled person into the public stocks because they might exhibit unusual behavior. These are examples of the down sides to obsolete forms of humiliation punishment that may have some applications to their modern counterparts.

There are many countries around the world where businesses use humiliation as a means of increasing employee productivity. In some places factory workers are made to wear embarrassing signs or oddly colored clothing to identify them as people who are not performing up to the standards of their fellow laborers. Poison pen memos and negative employee assessments sometimes replace those kinds of treatments in many western nations, but may be no less embarrassing or hurtful. Perhaps that is one of the reasons why workplace violence has become such a common occurrence.

I have no problem with humiliation as a means of humane punishment as long as it is not taken to extremes. In fact, it may be a partial solution to filling already dangerously over-crowded jails with people convicted of minor offenses. If it is being used as a means of embarrassing a child for something they said or wrote about a parent, I believe there are much better ways of dealing with those situations and that the use of humiliation in those cases is just the lazy parent's answer to dealing with conflicts they are unwilling to properly resolve.

There is a thin line between humiliation and bullying. When a parent does something to humiliate their child for disagreeing with them, they are essentially bullying them. It is part of a child's normal development to begin to question the wisdom of their parents, especially in the teen years. This is all part of the mental process that encourages a child to think for themselves and prepares them for the time when they will be on their own and have to make their own decisions and choices.

Parents have to use their own judgment when it comes to deciding when a child steps over the line in challenging them. Teens will always test the waters and see how far they can go before a parent yanks on the leash, but that doesn't mean that a parent should respond in kind with some outrageous act designed to embarrass their child. While humiliation may be a temporary fix to a conflict between a child and their parents, it is more likely to ramp up the situation than fix it in the long run. If the relationship between parents and their children is already a delicate balancing act, humiliation can push kids over the edge with sometimes tragic results.

Humiliation never gets to the root of the problem and should always be a last resort. if used at all, in parent and child relationships. Communication, conversation and explanation are better tools. Tell your child or teen what you expect from them and do not take 'No' for an answer. If they break the rules, find a punishment consummate with their infraction and act immediately. If your kids are using social networking in a manner that you find unacceptable, cut them off from it. It's dangerous to humiliate a child because, as we have learned from bullying, they might respond in a self-destructive manner like suicide and no one can take that back.

Chapter Ten: Parenting: Keeping Your Kids Safe From Child Predators

During the late 1970s I sat in a New York City courtroom waiting to be a witness for a friend of mine who was involved in a tenant-landlord dispute. The location was Manhattan and the entire scene reminded me of what you see when you watch those courtroom scenes from TV cop and crime shows. It really did look just like what we all see on TV and that really blew my mind. However, what happened next really freaked me out and has stuck in my memory from then to now.

Being from New York City, I was used to waiting my turn for everything. It's always been just a part of life for the millions of folks that live in the Big Apple and surrounding areas. Court is no different. The only good news was that most of the judicial proceedings ahead of us that day were either short legal housekeeping sessions or prearranged plea deal sentencing hearings. It was like court on speed dial. After less than two hours there was just one case ahead of us.

As that proceeding started, a well-dressed business woman came forward along with her lawyer. I thought this was probably some building code violation or traffic offense. I was stunned to the core when the prosecutor announced that the woman had been charged with child molestation.

The incident occurred aboard a commuter jet at a local airport. Due to in-climate weather, the aircraft was forced to wait for several hours before it was able to taxi to the deplaning platform.

During the delay, the woman allegedly molested a twelve year old girl sitting in a seat next to her. Only one witness saw it happen because the plane was mostly empty and the incident occurred late at night. If it were not for an attentive flight attendant, the incident would never have been noticed. She kept checking on the two because she though it was odd that the woman had invited the child to sit next to her. The attendant was walking past at one point and happened to notice that the woman had her hand stuck up inside the child's skirt. She alerted the flight crew and they notified the police.

Despite what I would think was the seriousness of the charges against her, the businesswomen had a wide smile on her face as her lawyer made an explanation for her behavior. The lawyer said that she was tired and stressed out from what turned out to be a long flight and an additional wait to deplane. The stress caused her to make a bad choice that she claims she did not even recall making. The child, traveling alone, later told her parents that she and the woman were just hugging to stay warm in a chilly plane.

In the end, the charges were dismissed and the well-dressed business woman walked out of the courtroom, free to molest again. I was stunned. So stunned that I'm sure I sounded a bit incoherent when my friend's turn came up. It took me hours to wrap my head around the fact that a woman was able to molest a young girl on an airplane at a major airport and simply walk out of a New York City courtroom with no consequences.

Things have changed quite a bit from those days. I'm almost certain that a scene like the one I witnessed in court back then would probably not occur very often in the now. However, the incident still sticks with me, not just because there was no penalty for the predator, but because the well-dressed business woman just didn't look like a typical child molester to me. I always pictured that kind of person as some nasty looking guy who bought pedophile magazines at some sleezy peep show parlor and hung around playgrounds looking for his next victim.

While I was growing up child predators were like town drunks. Lots of neighborhoods had one and your parents always told you never to go near that person's house for any reason. They were reluctantly tolerated because courts didn't want to send them to jail and no one else could figure out exactly what to do with them. I now believe that it was those many years of tolerating or ignoring these kinds of people that allowed their ranks to swell. However, the problem goes much deeper than that.

You would think that with all the laws that now protect kids from predators most anyone who had those kinds of sick thoughts swelling through their brains would not dare to try to act out their fantasies. The opposite seems to be true and the numbers don't lie. We have tens of thousands (or more) registered sex offenders here in the good old USA and their numbers are growing by the day.

Just recently a number of former and present Hollywood celebrities admitted that they had been molested, raped, abused or made to feel uncomfortable by failed attempts at those kinds of behavior by powerful people working in the entertainment industry. All of them say that this has been part of the status quo in Tinseltown for years. The only problem is that no one wants to name names. To do so, the celebrities claim, would permanently damage the industry.

The sad truth is that child predators are often protected by the very people they attack. Their victims just do not want to take them on for fear of embarrassment or public ridicule. There's also the chance the predator will be found not guilty or let go due to a lack of evidence. In many cases victims wait so long that legal statutes of limitations kick in and they cannot be charged under any criminal circumstances.

The recent allegations of child rape and molestation against figures in the sports world go to the very heart of the problem. The accused are married, have children and just do not seem to be the types of individuals that would commit these kinds of acts. These situations expose the best weapon that child predators have against being caught. They hide in traditional marriages, normal relationships and behind the facade of being successful and responsible community members. In short, they are wolves in sheep's clothing.

What really mystifies me is how we got to this point? Why are there so many child predators and molesters out there in our society? I believe that the answer lies in the fact that the entertainment and fashion industries have helped to fuel that fire without accepting any of the blame. It wasn't that many years ago that you could go to the movies and see naked children on the screen or walk into a book store in most any mall and buy books filled with nude photos of kids. All this was excused in the name of freedom of artistic expression.

Even today with far less nude scenes involving kids under eighteen in films, many movies still feature children involved in all sorts of sexual situations. Ads with kids acting or dressed in provocative ways still permeate society. However, those creating these kinds of films and ads are not the only offenders. At some point we have to blame ourselves because those kinds of films wouldn't be made unless people went to see them and those kinds of ads would not be out there if people refused to buy the things being hawked by scantily glad children and teens.

Don't misunderstand me. I fully understand and appreciate the fact that you cannot legislate morality. Lots of towns closed up their x-rated theaters and threw the pornography shops and peep shows out of town. It made things look better, but now all that any of the people that patronized those places have to do is go online. If you try to restrict pornography online (apart from child porn), you run the risk of starting politically-motivated social witch hunts. Every time some government agency restricts what we can do or say for what they claim is our own good, we end up losing valuable and irreplaceable freedoms.

I have a better idea and believe that one of the greatest weapons we have against child predators is personal responsibility. It's about protecting our kids. Parents and relatives must act in a preemptive way to keep their kids safe. If that means keeping them from being alone with people that we're supposed to trust, than that's the price of keeping them safe. Remember, child predators gravitate to employment and volunteer situations that give them the opportunity to be alone with and molest kids.

I have often wondered why, in the times we live in, any adult authority figure would be allowed to be alone with a child or teen. It's time to consider the use of paid or volunteer chaperones for situations that require kids to be alone or in close quarters with adults that might pose a threat to them. Yes it would cost something, but I wonder what the final bill will be at the universities where people have been recently accused of abusing and molesting kids on campus? I'm sure that the lawsuits will go on for years and end up costing tens of millions of dollars.

It's all well and good to pass laws and jail offenders, but the jails in many places are busting at the seams. None of this has done anything to stop not yet identified predators from harming children. We have to stop thinking about solving the problem after it has already occurred and start protecting our kids from situations that they may be intellectually and physically unable to deal with by being proactive. Let's not allow them to fall into the hands of predators to begin with.

We have to do more than lecture children about stranger danger. We have to look for the signs that a predator may be in our midst. Here are a few of the danger signals:

- An adult frequently wants to be alone with a child.

- An adult invites them over their house for extended periods of time or sleep overs.

- An adult readily and willing offers to babysit for a specific child on a regular basis.

- An adult gives money or gifts to a child without good reason.

- An adult offers to have a child do work for them regularly at a high rate of pay.

- An adult spends time with a child on their computer showing them unusual web sites.

- An adult shows a child or teen naked art, child pornography or films with nude children.

- An adult has too much physical contact with a child (frequent hugs or play wrestling).

- An adult regularly encourages a child to remove any part of their clothing for any reason.

- An adult offers to take a child on an overnight trip or camping for days at a time.

- An adult allows neighborhood kids regular access to his or her home as a meet up or play place.

It's not just adults we need to worry about. Many child predators begin molesting other children while they are kids themselves. Teach your children to watch out for kids that encourage their friends, playmates or peers to get naked in front of them or try to touch them in private areas of their bodies. These kinds of activities are likely to occur when adults are not around, so beware of your children playing over a house when no adult supervision is available. Kids that host what seem like a large number of sleep overs with many different friends or classmates should also be considered a possible threat. What might seem like innocent curiosity on the part of children can grow into something far worse. We have to make sure our kids do not do these kinds of things or allow themselves to be put at risk by other children that do.

If we all work together to take away the opportunity that predators have to attack kids, we cut off their supply of victims and begin to chip away at the heart of the problem. I believe that the number of possible child predators is growing because they have so many opportunities to attack and take advantage of kids. Take away these opportunities and at least some of these malefactors will think twice before acting out their fantasies.

Epilogue

I am always adding new information, free articles and ebooks to my web site. Please visit me online at http://jsi4.tripod.com where I trust you will find many helpful resources and the information you need to help Make Life Work For You...

Thank you for passing my way. I hope the information that I have provided has been helpful. If you would like to ask a question or make a comment, please feel free to email me at makelifeworkforyou@gmail.com

- Bill Edwards, 2012

www.ingramcontent.com/pod-product-compliance
Lightning Source LLC
Chambersburg PA
CBHW071600170526
45166CB00004B/1742

* 9 7 8 1 4 7 7 4 7 9 5 0 6 *